Your Goals This Year

A Year-by-Year Guide to
Homeschooling High School

Lee Binz,
The HomeScholar

First Printing, 2017

Printed in the United States of America

Cover Design by Robin Montoya
Edited by Kimberly Charron

ISBN: 1546977988
ISBN-13: 978-1546977988

Your Goals This Year

A Year-by-Year Guide to Homeschooling High School

What are Coffee Break Books?

Your Goals this Year is part of The HomeScholar's Coffee Break Book series.

Designed especially for parents who don't want to spend hours and hours reading a 400-page book on homeschooling high school, each book combines Lee's practical and friendly approach with detailed, but easy-to-digest information, perfect to read over a cup of coffee at your favorite coffee shop!

Never overwhelming, always accessible and manageable, each book in the series will give parents the tools they need to tackle the tasks of homeschooling high school, one warm sip at a time.

Everything about these Coffee Break Books is designed to suggest simplicity, ease, and comfort—from the size (fits in a purse), to the font and paragraph length (easy on the eyes), to the price (the same as a Starbucks Venti Triple Caramel Macchiato). Unlike a fancy coffee drink, however, these books are guilt-free pleasures you will want to enjoy again and again!

Table of Contents

Introduction

Know the Five Stages of Homeschooling High School

Many homeschool parents today are intimidated by the thought of homeschooling through high school, overwhelmed by the thought of college applications, and unsure how to plan for this final stage of their children's education. Generally, parents tend to react in one of two ways to this challenge. Some are stressed out; they need minimal information, because if they are given too much information, they become immobilized and can't do anything. On the complete opposite end of the spectrum are parents who need more and more information to overcome these challenges. These are the parents who want all of the information, all at one time, as soon as humanly possible. When they don't get it, they get incredibly stressed and frustrated.

Both kinds of parents need information in order to succeed at homeschooling high school, but one kind needs a ton, and the other kind needs to know when to plug their ears and hum, "La la la, I can't hear you!" No matter which kind of homeschool parent you are, knowing the five stages of homeschooling high school will put you on the path to success and help you keep from being overwhelmed.

The first stage of homeschooling high school is middle school, grades seven and eight (and sometimes grades six through eight), which is usually about ages twelve to thirteen. This is a time when you're training students in good study habits, grounding them in the basics, and helping them to explore what is starting to interest them.

Freshman year is next, which is grade nine, beginning at about age fourteen or fifteen. This is when keeping records and transcripts becomes important, because you'll be submitting them to colleges when your student applies in their senior year.

Next comes sophomore year, which is grade ten, about ages fifteen or sixteen. This is a time when you need to work on college preparation, such as making sure you are covering the courses most colleges require for admittance.

The next stage is junior year, eleventh grade, beginning at age sixteen or seventeen. This is the time to work on finding colleges your student is interested in, and going on campus visits.

Finally comes senior year, grade 12, at about ages 17 to 18. Senior year is when your student applies to any colleges of their choice, and gets ready to graduate.

The important point is to focus on what stage you are in, what's coming up, and to avoid the temptation to get overwhelmed by the big picture! Step-by-step, you can successfully homeschool high school!

The easiest way to determine grade level is to decide what year your child will be graduating from high school, and then count backwards. In other words, if your child is graduating next spring, this is the senior year. If your child is graduating a year from next spring, then your child is a junior this year.

The only time grade level *truly* matters is when they take the PSAT for real. They will ask your child for their grade level, and only the eleventh grade PSAT counts for National Merit Scholarships. (Your child can take it in tenth for fun, but only the eleventh grade level counts for scholarships.) Otherwise, it's all about when the child will graduate.

Summary of Ages and Grade Levels

The standard ages and grade levels for high school children may be helpful.

Freshman, grade 9, begins at age 14-15
Sophomore, grade 10, begins at age 15-16

Junior, grade 11, begins at age 16-17
Senior, grade 12, begins at age 17-18

But do standard age and grade levels matter? Not always—it depends on the child and the family. And sometimes it depends on the grade level of their friends, too.

When you are making the decision about graduation, keep in mind the magic number: 18. When children turn 18, they usually want to become independent. This is a good thing, because we have worked our entire lives to create independent, confident, capable young adults. The problem is that an independent, confident, capable young adult may not want to be homeschooled by Mommy. This can result in stress and difficulty at home, with even the most pleasant and compliant child. Without the agreement of the child, it may not be possible to homeschool a child over the age of 18 without some angst or drama at home.

Chapter 1

Middle School

Middle school, or junior high, is a great time for both homeschool parents and their students to get ready for high school! During seventh and eighth grades (or sixth, seventh and eighth grades), parents should be spending time learning how to homeschool high school. Take classes on homeschooling high school at a convention (or online), read books on how to homeschool high school, and visit the College Board website to see their college prep plan. In addition, junior high is the time to practice your record-keeping skills. You can practice making your transcript and writing course descriptions. This will prevent you from panicking when you get to the high school years!

Junior high has purpose for students, too. The first purpose is to allow them to do remedial work where needed. If they are below grade level in math, for instance, junior high is the time for them to focus on math and get up to grade level. Children who are ahead of grade level can move straight into high school level work. A student might be remedial in some areas, and advanced in others, so both of these situations might apply to the same student. The good news about junior high is that it's absolutely impossible for you to be behind. If your child is below grade level and they're in seventh or eighth grade, then the purpose of seventh or eighth grade is to get them up to grade level. You haven't done anything wrong and you're exactly where you should be.

Another goal for middle school is to continue to cultivate your child's love of reading. Reading truly is the gateway to learning and creating a passion and hunger for reading can cover a multitude of homeschooling sins. If your child is a voracious reader in middle school and high school, I guarantee you will be shocked about how much knowledge they have acquired by the time they graduate. In Appendix 1, I have compiled a great middle school reading list, that you can take to the library, to help encourage your children to read good books. Don't forget to read aloud to ease their development as lovers of literature. It also has the added benefits of promoting family bonding and ensuring better comprehension as you discuss the books you are reading together.

Beyond the Basics

If you're ready to go beyond the basics of junior high, you can start planning your high school courses. Get a rough draft started, including English, math, science, and social studies each year, and consider beginning to study a foreign language. This is also a great time to begin establishing excellent study skills in your kids so they understand what will be required in high school.

Lastly, junior high is a good time to investigate college financing. Learn about the different investment plans available, try to start setting money aside now, and estimate the financial aid that your child might receive. Use the FAFSA forecaster (FAFSA.ed.gov), which will help you estimate how much financial aid colleges might provide. Prepare now for high school, and the high school years will be so much easier!

Early High School Credits Earned in Middle School

If you are sure your child is doing high school level work in an academic subject area such as math, science, or foreign language, put it on their transcript so they earn early high school credits!

Why? Because when it's honest and true it goes on the transcript. And because schools do this, too!

I stumbled upon the Frederick County Public Schools website describing their policy.

"HIGH SCHOOL CREDIT EARNED IN MIDDLE SCHOOL

The Maryland State Board of Education allows local boards of education to grant graduation credit to middle school students who take high school courses in middle school. These courses must have the same expectations, curriculum and final exams as the equivalent courses taught in high school. The following FCPS middle school courses have been identified for high school credit:

- Algebra 1
- Geometry
- World Language levels 1 & 2 (i.e. German 1, 2, Spanish 1, 2, Latin 1, 2, French 1, 2, etc.)

Students who pass these courses and the final exam will automatically be granted high school credit. These grades will be reflected on the student's high school transcript and included in cumulative GPA calculations."

According to an article in The Columbus Dispatch a couple of years ago, "Middle-schoolers get additional shots at taking high-school courses," in Hilliard, eighth graders are eligible to take classes for high school credit, including science, math, and foreign language.

Chapter 2

Freshman Year

Whether you think they will go to college or not, if you have a freshman, make sure you provide them with a college prep education—just in case. Teenagers occasionally change their minds, and although they may think they don't want to go to college when they're younger, they might change their minds when they turn eighteen. If they do want to go to college, then a college prep education is important, because it will help them earn admission and be prepared academically. If they don't ultimately go to college, that's fine too, because your college prep plan will be their only formal education, so you want it to be a good one. It doesn't hurt anyone to be prepared.

Freshman year is the time to learn even more about how to homeschool high school. Take some classes, read some books, and find out what courses are required by colleges for admission. The most important thing to focus on is the core—reading, writing, math, history, and science.

This is also the time to be keeping records. There are two kinds of records that are essential for homeschooling high school: a reading list and a transcript. Keeping a reading list can be as easy as handing your child a piece of notebook paper or pointing them to a file on the computer, saying, "Every time you read a book, list the book here." Reading lists consist of the title and author of each book, nothing fancier or complicated at all. The second important record for freshman year, the transcript, doesn't have to be started until the spring, because sometimes your plans will change midyear and you won't finish a class, or will decide that Latin isn't right for your child and drop it. You don't need to include these changes in your transcript at all, so sometimes I recommend that parents work on transcripts in the spring.

Foreign Language

If you're ready to think beyond the basics of freshman year, consider foreign language, because it can be difficult for parents to get foreign language instruction in before kids graduate. Think about foreign language and ask yourself, "When are we going to take it? What year? How are we going to take it? What are we going to use?"

It's also a good time to review college prep plans to make sure you have the overall big picture. You don't want to need to cram three years of foreign language into one year. Spread everything out, so you have a good handle on the whole four-year high school plan. Freshman year is the time to get up to speed on all these details!

Testing

Your child's freshman year is the time to begin learning about high school testing. It's important to start thinking about this during freshman year because some tests are best administered to a child immediately after they finish a class. For instance, if they're studying chemistry and you decide you want them to take an AP test in chemistry, they should take the test right after they've learned the content.

You also need to decide whether your child should take an SAT, AP, or CLEP subject test. Some colleges only accept certain tests, so it's important to find out which ones are accepted by the colleges your child will most likely be attending. And don't forget to register for the tests so they can take them, because all the research in the world won't help if you don't register for the test! To register, all you have to do is call your local public or private high school and say, "I'm a homeschool parent, and would like to know if my homeschooled child can take the SAT or the AP subject test at your high school, and how do I register for it?" You can learn more about CLEP testing on the College Board website.

Colleges

It doesn't hurt to begin looking at colleges with your teenager now. You can identify a primary list of colleges you might consider. If you've always thought, "Probably these four are the ones we will apply to." or "My child has always mentioned an interest in going to Harvard." then you should begin to look at these colleges.

If you do have some colleges in mind, it's a good idea to look into their application requirements now, because if the college your child wants to attend is the one college in a million that requires four years of foreign language or something similarly unique, you need to know early in freshman year. You could also consider a college visit in the spring. Most college visits are done during the spring of junior year, but it's perfectly fine to take your children for college visits in freshman year or even earlier.

Encourage your freshman student to read and engage in activities. Begin to keep a reading list, and look into suggested books for the college-bound. Maintain an activity list filled with what your child is doing each year. This will help when, several years from now, you fill out a college application and the school asks, "What were you involved in for the last four years of high school?" If you keep an activity list, you'll remember what your child was involved in!

If you're feeling comfortable with freshman year, you may want to consider starting your course descriptions. It can be difficult to pull course descriptions together immediately before applying to college. If you have to write three years of course descriptions in one sitting, it could be tough. It's much, much easier to work on course descriptions one year at a time.

For help with course descriptions, check out my Comprehensive Record Solution at ComprehensiveRecordSolution.com

Chapter 3

Sophomore Year

Sophomore year is a good time to take the PSAT just for fun. It doesn't count for the National Merit Scholarship (that's junior year); it's merely for practice. The PSAT is only offered in October, so register for the test by September. It's easy to register: call your local public or private high school, and ask them if you can register your child to take the PSAT at their school.

If, for some reason, the high school says no, call the next closest high school. Most of them are very welcoming. The College Board is the company that oversees the PSAT, and they encourage public high schools to provide the tests for homeschooled children.

Good Records

As your child begins high school, make sure you're keeping good records. Keep a good reading list and work on your child's transcript each year. You might be asked to provide a transcript when you least expect it. For instance, when your child starts driving, and you want to get the "Good Student Discount," the insurance company will probably ask for a transcript. This can save you hundreds of dollars, so make sure you have it ready.

It's important to begin writing course descriptions early in high school. Don't be intimidated; they're each simply a paragraph about what the class was like. You're perfectly capable of writing them, but if you put it off until later, such as the first day of senior year, it will be difficult to come up with four years of course descriptions all at once.

Extra Credit

Some homeschool parents need to focus on completing the basics during their children's high school years, because that's all they can handle. Other parents are anxious to do it all and are ready for extra credit! If you are comfortable with homeschooling high school and want to learn more, here is what you can begin to focus on now, during your student's early years of high school.

Sophomore year is a great time to make sure you understand all about high school tests. Now is the time to ask yourself, "Which test is better for my child, the SAT or the ACT?" It's easy to obtain sample tests for the SAT and ACT. Have your student take a sample of each test, in your home, and then compare the scores to see which one makes your child look smarter. It's as easy as that, and nobody but you will ever know the results.

Once you've determined which test is best, begin studying for the SAT or ACT. Sophomore year is a good time to start studying, although you don't want to be too intense about it or stress your child out. Usually, if parents are ready to go beyond the basics, so are their children. Sophomore year is also a good time for your child to take subject tests, such as the SAT Subject Tests or AP subject tests, if these are necessary for your child. Some colleges require them, and it can be difficult to cover them all in senior year, so it's much easier to do a couple tests every year.

College

Sophomore year is a good time to think about college and college financing. Your child can start writing essays to apply for scholarships, and you can use these essays as your writing plan this year for English credit.

Sophomore year is a good time to get a jump on what kind of colleges you and your child are interested in. If possible, take your sophomore to a college fair. Visiting colleges is a good idea during sophomore year. Spend some time reading college catalogs. Think about what colleges want from homeschooled children, and ask the representatives at college fairs. Colleges may have requirements such as, "From homeschooled children, we prefer the ACT instead of the SAT." This is important information to learn, before it's hard to comply!

Chapter 4

Junior Year

Homeschooling high school is a lot of work at times, and junior year is definitely one of those times. More is required to prepare your student for college admission and scholarships during junior year than during freshman and sophomore year combined. If you have not been paying attention during those first two years, now is the time!

There are specific tasks you need to take care of during junior year to get yourself in a good place for senior year. First, you have to make sure that your child takes the PSAT. Taking this test during October of junior year is when it counts for the National Merit Scholarship program. If you have a smart child, taking the PSAT could save you thousands and thousands of dollars on college costs, so you don't want to miss it.

If your child isn't scoring high enough on tests to get a National Merit Scholarship, it's still important to take the PSAT during junior year because it's the perfect practice for both the SAT and the ACT. Your child will be taking this test in a public environment with other children around, filling in the bubbles for three hours, and there isn't a more perfect representation of what the SAT test is like than the PSAT.

College Fairs and Visits

Another important activity during junior year is to attend a college fair. This is absolutely critical for junior year. Going to a college fair is worth a trip to your nearest large city; it's worth a trip to visit Grandma; it's worth a trip to the local hub. Get to a college fair and meet as many colleges as possible in the shortest amount of time, all under one roof!

Spend some time reading about and comparing colleges after you attend the college fair. Which colleges were interesting? There might be thirty colleges you read about and compare in detail using a college reference book, which you will then try to whittle down into a more manageable list of six to ten colleges.

The next task is to visit colleges. This can be time consuming! My husband took a week off work and we visited one college close to home every day. If you are thinking about sending your child a long way from home, it's even more important to visit that college, so you'll know whether it's a place you want your child to live.

SAT and ACT

One of the major jobs for homeschoolers in eleventh grade is to decide whether to take the SAT or ACT. It's important to choose the test that makes your child look like a genius. In order to make an informed choice, give your child a sample of each test. You can get free sample tests at college fairs or online. Giving the test at home under a low-stress situation will help you find out which one is better for your child.

Before they take the test, your student should study. If they plan to take an AP or SAT Subject Test exam, they should study for them as well. Spring of junior year is when most students take college admission tests, and I usually recommend taking them early in the spring, such as in March. This way, if your child has a bad day, broke their arm the night before, or woke up in the morning with the flu and couldn't go, they still have an opportunity to take the tests in May or June.

One of the reasons it's so important to take these tests in spring of junior year is so you have scores handy to determine which colleges are appropriate for your student. You also want to submit nice-looking scores when you apply to colleges during senior year, so you need to have this information ahead of time.

Records

Another task of junior year is to keep records, because this is when it's important. Soon you will be turning your child's records in to colleges. You don't want to forget anything, and you certainly don't want to wait until the last moment and create a transcript the week before it's due in senior year.

The records you need to keep include a transcript with each course title and course grade, a reading list which is simply a list of books your child has read for school or for fun, course descriptions that include what you used to teach the class and how you graded, and an activity and awards list. One of the biggest questions asked on a college application is what the student is involved in, and it's hard to remember off the top of your head.

Strategies for College Success

One of the best ways to save on college costs is to be prepared ahead of time. During your child's junior year, you can become prepared for college success by learning about the college admission process, helping your student develop strong essay writing skills, and focusing on SAT or ACT test preparation. If you cover these areas, you will have more time and energy to focus on extra college preparations, which can lead to scholarships and savings.

Sometime before senior year, consider CLEP exams. CLEP exams are subject exams that can be used for college credit. If your child passes a CLEP exam, it could save you thousands of dollars on college costs, so it's worth looking into.

Homeschoolers often focus on urgent subjects, such as math or spelling, or "Oh my gosh, we're out of time! I've got to get to foreign language!" But you also need to remember to teach what's important for the long term.

Now that my children are older, I recognize that teaching worldview is extremely important. Students who study worldviews are less likely to get blown out of the water in terms of their beliefs when they're in college. Encouraging a good work ethic is also important, because all of the education in the world won't matter much if your student doesn't have a strong work ethic. They have to learn to stick it out for four years of college, or that tuition money won't result in a diploma.

It's amazingly important for college preparation to understand the importance of sleep. The number one problem kids have adjusting to college is that they don't get enough sleep. Time management is also important to teach, since your child will be responsible for their own time at college. Rather than watching them fail at time management, teach them the skills they will need for college success now.

Last on the important-to-learn-for-college list is the ability to write a college style essay. This is something my children have thanked me for teaching them. We covered this in high school, because it was part of the SAT and the ACT test. Of course, essays are important for life, too, because even if you don't take the SAT test, a lot of college is about writing, from essay tests to a one-page paper that's due tomorrow. Even in the work world, it's important to be able to write quickly. Adults sometimes need to get Christmas letters done, write thank you notes, apply for a job, or explain responsibilities at the last job, so being able to write is an important life skill.

Planning Ahead

If you're the kind of parent who is not overwhelmed by high school and college preparation, and wants even more information, there is more you can do ahead of time during your child's junior year to prepare them for success in college.

During junior year, it's a good idea to plan ahead for college admission as much as possible. While this may be difficult, it can become more difficult when your child is a senior, for two reasons. First, seniors often become overcommitted, and may be too busy to do anything during the year. Second, they can become independent adults when they're seniors, and might not want Mom telling them what to do—even when they know it's the right thing to do. There is the possibility your teenager will put up a brick wall and balk during senior year, so if you are on top of things during junior year, you can avoid some of the stress.

Planning ahead during junior year means completing one or two college applications, and saving them for later. Track down one or two colleges your child is most likely to want to go to, and have them fill out those college applications. Practice filling out applications is a great exercise. It can help them see why you've been so focused on math or foreign language for the last two years, when they see how important it is to colleges.

You can also plan ahead by assigning your student a college application essay, which you can find on the application. This can help when senior year comes, because if your student gets too busy and doesn't have time to write essays (perhaps because of a full time job and a full course load), you'll still have the option of turning in what they completed during junior year.

Plan ahead, and I guarantee life will be much easier!

Chapter 5

Senior Year

Senior year is a busy time in a homeschooler's life, for both parent and student. There's so much to do! For those who are planning to attend college, senior year is all about applying, and there are many steps in that process, so preparation is key. For the best results, you want to hit the ground running during this last year of high school.

College Applications

It's not too early to begin filling out college applications on the very first day of senior year. In fact, if your student is doing dual enrollment (both high school and college), during senior year, it will help if you start applications before school starts. College applications can be complicated; they involve technically perfect, self-reflective essays, which are difficult and take lots of time. See Appendix 1 for more strategies for dual enrollment/community college success.

Applications also include complex forms, with lots of questions, and require letters of recommendation. To get recommendation letters, you must brainstorm who to ask, and then you have to ask them, and for some reason, it takes kids quite a bit of time to work up the nerve to ask somebody to write them a letter of recommendation. They need to allow a lot of time for each person to write the recommendation, and you have to allow some time for them to mail it directly to the college. As you can see, getting a letter of recommendation does not happen overnight; it takes lots of planning ahead.

Applying for college is remarkably like filling out your federal tax forms for April 15th. There are firm deadlines with strange expectations, a whole bunch of fine print, words you don't understand,

and if you mess up, there's a huge financial consequence in the end. Plan ahead and spend time on it, making sure you start on the first day of senior year.

Fill Gaps

Another important task during senior year is to fill any gaps you identify. You can repeat tests if your student needs to improve SAT/ACT scores. If you find any major educational gaps, you can catch up during senior year. If, for example, you haven't started the foreign language class required by the college your student wants to attend, you could have them take foreign language at a community college. One year of foreign language at community college is equal to two or three years of high school foreign language, so it can be a way to quickly fill a gap. Take this opportunity to make sure your senior has all the requirements he needs before graduation, and plan ahead as much as possible.

Records

Senior year is the most critical time for you to complete high school records, because you have to turn in the transcript when you turn in college applications. Include the classes your child is currently taking. If they're taking Pre-Calculus during senior year, then put Pre-Calculus on the transcript, but instead of a grade, enter To Be Determined (TBD) or In Progress/In Process (IP). This shows that your child is in the process of completing the class, and will be finished in June. Have the transcript ready to go early in senior year, so you can send it to colleges along with applications early in the fall.

Most colleges ask for additional materials besides a transcript, so have your child's reading list ready, too. I also strongly suggest you check out samples and quick shortcuts to make course descriptions in the least stressful way at The HomeScholar website.

Although a transcript is required in the fall when your child applies to college, you must still send in their final transcript in the summer after your student graduates in June. You will be asked for the final transcript by the college, including your student's final grades.

Way Behind

What can you do when you have a senior and you're way behind? I know that sometimes parents are happily homeschooling a handful of children and then all of a sudden, they realize, "Oh my gosh! I have a senior, and I have no idea!" I know this can happen!

Put together a college prep plan and a college planning guide, and start checking off classes, considering "What have we done? What haven't we done? Where are the gaps? Have we done economics? Have we done fine arts?" Identify and fill the gaps, those missing, recommended classes. You can easily do so if you check at the beginning of senior year.

Filling in missing classes is something I had to do with my own children. One son loves economics, and that was all he ever wanted to study during his high school years. However, when I went through my other son Kevin's courses, and checked off his classes on my planning guide, I realized I had forgotten to teach him economics! It can happen to anybody.

Then, have your child take the next available SAT or ACT test. Don't worry about which test to take; at this point, you can't be choosy. Register your child for the next available test.

Next you need to make a transcript. This may seem like an overwhelming task if you haven't started your transcript yet, but you can take a few online classes and sit down and create a rough draft for your transcript as quickly as possible. It may not be the perfect transcript, but it will be good enough for you to turn in during the first few months of senior year.

If you can, attend a college fair. You can Google "college fair your city" and see what you come up with. Then it's time to apply to colleges. Simply do your best. Locate two public and two private universities, ones closest to you and ones you and your child both approve of. If you've never thought about college before and you haven't planned through senior year, then I don't recommend applying to a competitive school. Consider general public or private universities, and apply to two each. Hopefully your child will get some scholarships if you apply early. Even if you haven't planned out senior year, your child might earn scholarships simply by applying early. Later in the year, take more time to look at other colleges to see whether there are any you're interested in. The information from your early applications can be used in later ones.

Beyond the Basics

If you're comfortable with senior year, I encourage you to look beyond the basics.

If you are stressed out, don't read this next section!

First, position yourself for maximum financial aid. Apply to colleges early and often. This morning, I got an email from a college saying, "If you apply by October 12th, we'll give you an additional $3,000 for financial aid." Merely for applying earlier than their early deadline, they give more money! Their early deadline could still result in $20,000, and they were offering another $3,000 to people who applied earlier than the early deadline. Early and often does matter!

Watch deadlines and details, because sometimes colleges include unusual details, and ask for some strange things. Make sure you give them everything they need. If they ask you for a lab write-up from your child's high school biology class, submit it. If they ask for the transcript in an envelope, signed on the seal, do it!

If your child's information changes, update it with admissions. For instance, if you find out your child is a National Merit Scholar, or if they've been given a private scholarship for an essay they wrote during junior year, send the information on and say, "My student has just received this additional scholarship." This will put your student in an even better light and may result in more scholarships.

One of the most important things to remember beyond the basics is to expect three waves of scholarships. Here's how it works. When you apply for college, your child is given some immediate scholarships based on SAT or ACT scores, and their GPA. This will be a cause for partying, until you compare the scholarship and the cost of college and realize, "Hmm, we still can't afford college!" Fortunately, there is a second wave of scholarships based on the FAFSA and financial need. Although you complete the FAFSA in October of senior year, you don't learn about this wave of scholarships until much later in the year.

The third wave of scholarships is based on merit, or other qualities, and these scholarships may not arrive until May or June. For this reason, the most difficult time for parents is between March and June. You know what college your child wants to attend. You know that your child has been admitted. But because the financial aid hasn't all come in, you have absolutely no clue how you're going to pay for it! I encourage you to be patient until you get the final wave of scholarships between March and June.

Celebrate!

The next thing to do is plan a graduation celebration. This is for everybody! You can celebrate your senior whether you have an organized homeschool or not, because when children graduate, it is truly a cause for celebration. The best thing I can do is point you to HomeschoolDiploma.com, because you can get diplomas, invitations, thank you notes, honor cords, caps and gowns, and anything you need to announce the event there. They have suggested wording for announcements, and you can customize templates or completely change the words yourself.

You may want to schedule senior portraits, too. Sometimes people include their senior portrait on social media accounts and since potential employers often check an applicant's online presence, portraits can be useful.

It's time to celebrate! Remember to plan a graduation event, too. Some homeschoolers plan an event with their local homeschool group, and have a graduation ceremony, the same way public and private high schools do. Contact these organizations early in the winter or spring if you want to participate in their ceremonies, because they usually have a specific date in mind and tasks you need to complete before the date.

You can also celebrate at home, which is what we did. Simply hold a barbecue with family and friends. We served a buffet meal, and of course, graduation cakes. Since I had two graduates, I provided two graduation cakes.

We made memory boards to display for Kevin and Alex. Kevin was involved in chess, so his was decorated with chessboards. Alex was involved in public policy, but also loved the piano, so we put his on the piano. My nephew gave us a tip for a website to make a slideshow online, www.animoto.com. Upload pictures, add a few words, and the program will add the music and graphics for you.

I also purchased the book, *Oh, The Places You'll Go!* by Dr. Seuss. It's traditionally given to high school and college graduates, and we used it as their senior yearbook. Everybody who came to our party signed the book as if they were signing a high school yearbook; it was fun and a great memento for them.

Dramatic Changes

It's important to remember that there will be dramatic changes over the four years of high school. Maturity happens. The changes you saw in your child between the time they were a newborn and four years old are the same kind of dramatic changes that will occur between freshman and senior year. Don't be scared that your child won't ever mature enough to graduate, or that they'll never go off on their own! Huge changes take place between freshman and senior year, so don't give up hope!

Instead, be prepared, because teenagers do change their minds, and they may go back and forth between "I'm going to college" and "I'm never going to college; what a stupid idea." Situations can change. Be prepared in case your teenager balks during senior year.

Senior year is close to adulthood, and sometimes adults don't want to do what their mothers tell them to do! Be prepared when teenagers make adult decisions—when they become adults. Avoid fear that immobilizes you, and focus only on the goals for each year of high school. Before you know it, you'll be waving goodbye as your child heads off to college, and you'll wonder where the time went. Relax and enjoy each year's challenges and rewards!

Chapter 6

High School Graduation Checklist

Parents can provide college preparation during high school, which can benefit every child. If they ultimately don't go to college, then your homeschool education will be the only education they get. Make it great! They'll be well prepared for life and their civic responsibilities. Plus, if they ever change their mind and decide to go to college, they will have a much easier time getting in. On the other hand, some parents know early on that their children are college bound. For them, a college prep education can influence the quality of the colleges that accept them. College preparation can benefit everyone!

Plan Courses

During eighth and ninth grades, find out about your own state requirements and make a plan to meet them. Review the common college expectations for high school courses. For help with courses, see my Coffee Break Book on *Planning High School Courses.*

Look over your high school plan at least once a year. As you begin to focus on college and career goals, you may need to adjust your plan slightly each year as you go. Budding nurses and engineers may need to buckle down in math, and missionary preparation could benefit from more foreign language study. Try to include essay writing in your plan. The ability to write a few paragraphs quickly can be beneficial for both college and career dreams. Review your plan yearly while you relax and enjoy a lifestyle of learning.

Plan for Tests

High school testing can cause stress for parents *and* students. What test do you take when, and how do you know? Most of these answers are found on two websites: CollegeBoard.org and ACT.org.

Register your child for the PSAT in tenth grade for fun, but only the PSAT taken in eleventh grade counts toward the National Merit Scholarship. It's only offered once each year, so register before September of the student's junior year (in eleventh grade). College admission tests, the SAT and ACT, are often taken in eleventh grade and repeated if necessary.

Take some time to learn about additional subject tests to measure knowledge in specific areas. SAT Subject Tests are best taken immediately after your child completes each subject. For example, register your child for the SAT Subject Test in French after you finish studying French. Consider AP exams when you finish courses as well. They are more intensive subject tests, but they can earn your child college credit!

Extra-Curricular Activities

You want your kids to be well-rounded, and colleges want this, too! Encourage your child to volunteer for community service. Consider employment, internships, or apprenticeships. Encourage activities such as sports, music, and art. Colleges love to see passionate kids. They can see this elusive "passion" in extra-curricular activities that students continue through all four years of high school. The Washington Post suggests it's best to focus on one or two areas of specialization, rather than doing a little of everything.

Finding a College

Finding a college is more than considering where your friends and neighbors go to school. Take your sophomore or junior to a college fair, or search online for the perfect college match for your student. Once you discover some possibilities, visit each college in person. Visiting is the only way to see if it's a perfect match. Try to whittle down the list to a handful of colleges by the end of junior year. When you visit, ask about their homeschool admission policy. Find out what records they want from you and about any additional testing requirements. Consider getting my Coffee Break Book, *Finding a College*, for more detailed information.

Consider College Finances

You know you *should* be saving for college, but people certainly have varying degrees of success doing so! You can search for scholarships at any time, but if finances are a huge concern, you may want to work on a scholarship search during sophomore and junior years.

Don't be afraid of private schools. They often give significantly better financial aid than public schools, and this often makes tuition costs comparable. Forbes Magazine published an article, "The

World's Most Expensive Universities"
that explains:

"Those costs reflect a trend among
private American universities--
charge a stratospheric tuition fee,
then offer a generous financial aid
package."

So don't be afraid of the list price of a
school.

In October of senior year, parents
should complete the FAFSA. This IRS-
style form helps colleges determine how
much money the government thinks you
can afford to pay for college—often with
hilarious results! Here we are worrying
about the price of gasoline, and they
think we can afford that amount? The
FAFSA is used to determine how much
financial aid colleges will give your child.

Prepare High School Records

Once you decide where your child will
apply, ask these colleges what high
school records they require. It can vary
significantly, and there is no way to

know unless you ask. They may only ask for a transcript. Some colleges also request a simple reading list, but others want exhaustive course descriptions and grading criteria. Some colleges have strange and unique requirements. Find out their requirements early so you can give them what they want. This is why I always recommend keeping samples of everything in high school – you never know what they will want. One college asked me for a graded English paper . Another college wanted subject tests in many different areas. Like a boy scout, be prepared! At the end of the homeschooling journey, at the end of senior year, remember to send the college a final transcript that includes graduation date, final grades, and grade point average.

Apply to College

College applications are long and complicated. Admission essays are tedious and time consuming. Plan to begin the application process during September of senior year to allow enough time to complete it in a timely fashion. It's possible to write college application essays in junior year if you want to plan ahead. You can always edit it again right before submitting it. Start early. Each college may require two or more essays, and their application can be many more additional pages. Sometimes admission and financial aid decisions are "first come, first served" so it can pay off to plan ahead. I encourage students to finish applications by January first whenever possible, to be in the best possible position. The college deadline may be later, but they will be swamped with applicants near the deadline. They can give your application a more relaxed reading if you turn it in early.

Be Confident in the Benefits of Homeschooling

Homeschoolers have the advantage in college preparation! We are intimately involved in our children's education. We know their strengths and weaknesses, their goals and passions. We can provide the best guidance counseling for them because we are love-givers, not caregivers. In school settings, a guidance counselor may know a lot about tests and deadlines, that's true. But they have hundreds of students to help, and they may speak to each student only once or twice. Just like our wonderful student-teacher ratio, our student-advisor ratio can't be beat!

Be brave! Parents know their children better than anyone, and they are perfectly capable of providing the guidance they need through high school. You can do it!

Appendix 1

Middle School Reading List

All families are different and must decide their own standards for the books their children read. Parents assume all responsibility for their children's education. This book list is based on commonly recommended books for middle school students, heavily influenced by the reading we have done with our own children. If you are not familiar with something on this list, please review the book first. It's been a long time since I read them myself, as the parent of a middle school student, and only you know your child's maturity level.

If you have a reluctant reader, focus on short, classic books. For kinesthetic learners, focus on books with active main characters. For those voracious readers, feed their book hunger with quality literature instead of junk. For moody children, avoid dark characters or themes and locate uplifting books with heroes and over-comers. Middle school reading lists have become darker in our current educational system. For a fascinating comparison, see this article: Middle School Reading Lists 100 Years Ago vs. Today. (http://www.better-ed.org/blog/middle-school-reading-lists-100-years-ago-vs-today).

One resource that helped us choose books was *The Read Aloud Handbook*, by Jim Trelease.

The following books are generally suitable for middle schoolers, ages 11-13. For a printable reading list, go to: https://s3-us-west-2.amazonaws.com/hhhpdf/Middle-School-Reading-List.pdf

- Adams, Richard *Watership Down*
- Alcott, Louisa May *An Old-Fashioned Girl*
- Alcott, Louisa May *Little Women*
- Babbit, Natalie *Tuck Ever*lasting
- Barrie, J.M. *Peter Pan*
- Bendick, Jeanne *Archimedes and the Door of Science*
- Blackwood, Gary *The Shakespeare Stealer*
- Bolt, Robert *A Man for All Seasons*
- Bunyan, John *The Pilgrim's Progress*
- Burnett, Frances Hodgson *The Secret Garden*
- Carroll, Lewis *Alice's Adventures in Wonderland*
- Carroll, Lewis *Through the Looking-Glass*
- Cather, Willa *My Antonia*
- Chesterton, G.K. *The Ballad of the White Horse*
- Cohen, Barbara *Seven Daughters and Seven Sons*
- Collier, James Lincoln *My Brother Sam Is Dead*

- Cushman, Karen *Catherine, Called Birdie*
- Daugherty, James *The Magna Charta*
- Defoe, Daniel *Robinson Crusoe*
- De Angeli, Marguerite *The Door in the Wall*
- Dickens, Charles *A Christmas Carol*
- Doyle, Arthur Conan *The Red-headed League*
- Ellis, Deborah *The Breadwinner* (3 book series)
- Farley, Walter *The Black Stallion* series
- Fitzgerald, John D. *The Great Brain*
- Fletcher, Susan *Shadow Spinner*
- Forbes, Esther Hoskins *Johnny Tremain*
- Frank, Anne *The Diary of a Young Girl*
- Freedman, Russell *Freedom Walkers: The Story of the Montgomery Bus Boycott*
- George, Jean Craighead *My Side of the Mountain*

- George, Jean Craighead *Tree Castle Island*
- Gipson, Fred *Old Yeller*
- Grahame, Kenneth *The Wind in the Willows*
- Henty, G.A. *In Freedom's Cause*
- Holling, Holling Clancy *Paddle-to-the-Sea*
- Hunt, Irene *Across Five Aprils*
- Jacques, Brian *Redwall* Series
- Juster, Norton *The Phantom Tollbooth*
- Keith, Harold *Rifles for Watie*
- Kipling, Rudyard *Captain Courageous*
- Kipling, Rudyard *The Jungle Book*
- Konigsburg, E.L. *From The Mixed-Up Files of Mrs. Basil E. Frankweiler*
- L'Engle, Madeleine *A Wrinkle in Time* series
- Lawrence, Caroline *The Roman Mysteries*
- Lee, Harper *To Kill a Mockingbird*
- Lewis, C.S. *The Chronicles of Narnia*
- Lindgren, Astrid *Pippi Longstocking*

- London, Jack *The Call of the Wild*
- London, Jack *White Fang*
- Lowry, Lois *The Giver*
- Lowry, Lois *Number the Stars*
- MacDonald, George *The Princess and the Goblin*
- MacLachlan, Patricia *Sarah Plain and Tall*
- McGraw, Eloise Jarvis *The Golden Goblet*
- Montgomery, L.M. *Anne of Green Gables* series
- Moody, Ralph The Dry Divide
- Naylor, Phyllis Reynolds *Saving Shiloh*
- Paterson, Katherine *Bridge to Terabithia*
- Paulsen, Gary *Hatchet*
- Peretti, Frank E. *The Cooper Kids Adventure* series
- Polland, Madeleine *Beorn the Proud*
- Pope, Elizabeth Marie *The Sherwood Ring*
- Pyle, Howard *Men of Iron*
- Pyle, Howard *The Story of King Arthur and His Knights*

- Pyle, Howard *Otto of the Silver Hand*
- Pyle, Howard and McKowen, Scott *The Merry Adventures of Robin Hood*
- Rawlings, Marjorie *Kinnan The Yearling*
- Rawls, Wilson *Where the Red Fern Grows*
- Robinson, Barbara *The Best Christmas Pageant Ever*
- Rogers, Jonathan *The Wilderking Trilogy*
- Sewell, Anna *Black Beauty*
- Speare, Elizabeth George *The Bronze Bow*
- Speare, Elizabeth George *The Witch of Blackbird Pond*
- Stevenson, Robert Louis *The Black Arrow*
- Stevenson, Robert Louis *Kidnapped*
- Stevenson, Robert Louis *Treasure Island*
- Sutcliff, Rosemary *The Roman Britain* trilogy (*The Eagle of the Ninth*)
- Tolkien, J.R.R. *The Hobbit*

- Twain, Mark *Adventures of Huckleberry Finn*
- Twain, Mark The Adventures of Tom Sawyer
- Verne, Jules *Twenty Thousand Leagues Under the Sea*
- Verne, Jules *Around the World in 80 Days*
- Wallace, Lew *Ben-Hur*
- Washington, Booker T. *Up From Slavery*
- White, T.H. *The Sword in the Stone*
- Wilder, Laura Ingalls *The Little House* series
- Williamson, Joanne *Hittite Warrior*
- Wyss, Johann David *The Swiss Family Robinson*

Of course, reading is even more important for college-bound homeschoolers. I have created a college-bound reading list for high schoolers that you can find here:

HomeHighSchoolHelp.com/college-bound-reading-list

For a printable version of this list, please go here:

http://hhhpdf.s3.amazonaws.com/Colle ge-Bound-Reading-List.pdf

Appendix 2

Strategies for Community College Success

Are you considering dual enrollment but concerned about grades? Many homeschoolers are jumping into the fast track to college credits with community college because many states pay the tuition for qualified high school juniors and seniors. It's an attractive opportunity, but the transition can be stressful for parents and teens. All of a sudden, your high school student is taking college courses, so the work is more difficult and the grades feel so much more real, permanent, and significant. Have no fear! Let me explain how you can encourage your children to be successful in dual enrollment.

Six Tips for Maximum Benefit

1. Find out university policies on community college classes. You want to be sure how they will use college classes before your child transfers to a four-year university. Some universities will not accept certain community college courses. Other universities will consider your student a transfer applicant rather than a freshman applicant, which can affect scholarships. Some universities won't give credit but will use those classes to place your student in higher level courses. Do your research to locate a "dual enrollment policy" for any university your child is interested in attending, so you are prepared.

2. Have your child take a community college class in each major subject area. Try to cover at least one class in math, history, English, science, etc. For students who are taking a handful of classes, this will help you provide outside documentation of ability in a broad array of subjects. Instead of only proving their mettle in math, try to demonstrate abilities across the board.

Some teens will attempt a full course load at community college to achieve an Associate of Arts (AA) degree, which means covering all the subject areas to achieve that distinction.

3. Have your child take classes required by your first choice university. Then they won't need to repeat the same class when they transfer. This can shorten the time they stay in (and you need to pay for) college. For example, if your chosen university requires everyone to take a psychology class, taking psychology as a dual enrolled high school student can eliminate the need to take it at the university.

4. Be prepared for college applications after community college. Even if your child completes dual enrollment, when they want to attend a four-year college in the future, you'll still need complete high school records. Be ready to provide a transcript, course descriptions, reading list, and activity list. Collect course descriptions for classes taken at the community college, in case the

information is needed for a smooth transition.

5. Advise your teenager to get to know their professors. College professors are one of the best sources of letters of recommendation. For the best results, these professors should know your child well in order to write knowledgeably about them. Tell your children to sit in the front row, ask questions in class, and participate in discussions. This will help them get better grades, certainly, but it will also help professors get to know them.

6. Make sure your child gets excellent grades in all college classes. College grades weigh heavily in admission and scholarship decisions, even if a university does not give college credit for the classes. Emphasize the importance of getting excellent grades – hopefully all A's.

It's important for kids to do well in community college classes. These college grades will take priority over any high school grades on the transcript. When colleges look at grades, GPA, and SAT or ACT test scores, they are trying to predict who will be successful in college. What could be a better measurement of college success than documented success in college? College grades are the most accurate measurement of college readiness, so they should be good. However, you don't need to panic! While community college grades can affect college admission and scholarship opportunities, there are plenty of reasons not to worry.

Five Reasons Not to Worry about Grades

1. Most students drop a grade. Keep in mind that college classes are more difficult than high school classes and students will drop one whole grade level on average when they make the switch. In other words, an "A" student usually gets a "B"; a "B" student usually gets a "C."

2. Average homeschoolers tend to get excellent grades. Many homeschoolers get A's because, quite frankly, moms are

usually tougher on them than college professors. We expect our children to truly learn and achieve mastery over concepts. Learning and mastery are words that equal "good grades."

3. Hard work earns great grades. Give your children the expectation of working hard to get an "A" in every class. However, truth be told, if they get a "B" or better, they can still do well in the college admission process (depending on where they want to apply, of course).

4. Classes aren't filled with geniuses. Community college students are not all top-performing students. Adults returning to college and high school drop-outs will re-enter education through community college. The straight-A types generally go to a four-year university instead, so the competition isn't usually as tough as a regular four-year university. Even if professors grade on the curve, a smart homeschooler can typically out-score a moderate adult who hasn't taken English or math in the last few decades.

5. Homeschooled kids worry about comparisons. According to statistics, homeschoolers are wonderfully prepared for college. Still, kids may wonder if they have been well-educated by their parents and as a result are willing to work extra hard to prove they are educated.

Although your children may get terrific grades in college, the experience isn't only about the GPA. You want them to study and learn college material, not only be able to pass a test. You can guide your children so they can be successful in learning at the college level.

Seven Strategies for Community College Success

1. Read the syllabus carefully on the first day of class. The syllabus will explain all the requirements, assignments, and tests for the entire class. Put all deadlines on the calendar.

2. Plan for two hours of studying for every hour spent in class. This general formula will help you estimate the time

required for each class. Your children can read the book and circle, highlight, underline, discuss, make note cards, form a study group, etc.

3. Ensure your child attends class every single day. This isn't generally a problem for homeschoolers, who are never "absent" at home. However, it can be shocking to see how many students in college decide not to attend class. Most professors don't teach from a textbook and their lectures supplement the text. Class attendance is critical.

4. Teach your child how to take notes and be an active listener. This can help your student remain engaged in lectures and improve their retention. IEW has an excellent note-taking class, called the Advanced Communication Series. Your child can practice note-taking skills in church or while watching college level lectures from The Great Courses.

5. Suggest that your child sit at the front of the class. Professors know that students who sit at the front of class tend to be more engaged in learning.

This will encourage learning and retention, but it will also help your child develop a professional academic relationship. Hopefully the professor will be happy to write a marvelous letter of recommendation when the time comes.

6. Encourage your child to get help when needed. During the first day of class, the professor will explain how they can be reached for questions. It's important to ask for help immediately, when questions remain small, rather than waiting until the subject is overwhelmingly confusing. Remind your student to attend the professor's office hours (with another student) at the first sign of confusion. When speaking to a professor, there is no reason to reveal they are in high school, or in dual enrollment, or homeschooled. To the professor, each student is on equal footing.

7. Form a study group. Encourage your child to get to know other students in the class - especially anyone who also sits at the front of the class. They can

develop a study group, and meet together regularly. Because of the variety of students attending community college, the best way to develop a study group is with other homeschooled students, or at least with other students attending through dual enrollment. It is an adult environment, with some unsavory characters attending class, so be careful.

Homeschoolers need to be aware of the potential pitfalls, as well as the possibilities, of a community college education. These college credits may be free, but parents should do their research before sending children into the community college environment. One community college approached me at a college fair, and asked me to warn parents that their young homeschooled daughters may be sitting next to registered sex offenders, unaware of the danger. (For more information about the environment, read "Facing the Community College Fad" on my website.)

Even though it's up to your child to attend the classes and do the work, there are things parents can do to help their children have a successful community college experience.

Seven Things Parents Can Do to Help

1. Arrange a buddy system. Find other friends, perhaps other homeschoolers, who can attend class together. When our sons went to community college, they were in a classroom together or with another Christian friend.

2. Evaluate the professors. A good place to find helpful information is www.ratemyprofessors.com. Look at the comments as well as the ratings, because some students rate professors highly merely due to the fact they don't give homework, or show inappropriate material in class.

3. Preview the textbooks in advance. The textbook can give you a clue about the coming class, and perhaps give a sense of the professor's philosophical bent. My

son previewed the textbook for a music improvisation course and immediately proclaimed, "Mom, I can't take this class." I frankly thought he was just blowing off a little teenager steam, until I looked at the passages in the textbook that he pointed out. The author said that he would always capitalize the word "Self" throughout the book because, "You should always capitalize the name of God." He went on to say that since only God could create music, that meant you were, in fact, God. So check those textbooks and be prepared!

4. Avoid over-working your student. If your child is taking a full time community college course load, do not expect any additional homeschool classes. If your child is taking two full community college classes, they might be able to do one or two classes at home. If your child is taking one full community college class at a time, you might expect them to get about half of their usual homeschool workload completed.

5. Don't double up with homeschool classes. One whole college class equals one whole high school credit. This means, for instance, that a community college class in English is the only English class needed that year. On the other hand, it also means that a community college class goes faster than a high school class - twice as fast or more. (Check out my article, "Two for the Price of One," for more details.)

6. Withdraw from class if necessary. At most colleges, a student can withdraw from class within the first few days. This might be an option if you believe your child will be completely overwhelmed by the work listed in the syllabus, or if you decide the class content or professor is inappropriate.

7. Keep complete homeschool records. When your child is taking community college classes, you need to include that information on your homeschool transcript. Clearly indicate which classes were taken at the community college, using the college's acronym by each class title. For more information on

transcripts, take my free online class, "A Homeschool Parent's Guide to Grades, Credits, and Transcripts." If you need extra help creating your homeschool transcript, check out my Total Transcript Solution.

Do your research about dual enrollment, and make sure it's a good fit for your child. Even if your child gets good grades, there are other issues to consider. Community college can be a "Rated R" environment. Read my article, "Facing the Community College Fad" to help make your decision.

Community college success is attainable and it can be a great and rewarding experience! Your child will be well prepared for university and those classes will be a great help in paving the way for college admission and scholarships.

Afterword

Who is Lee Binz and What Can She Do for Me?

Number one best-selling homeschool author, Lee Binz is The HomeScholar. Her mission is "helping parents homeschool high school." Lee and her husband Matt homeschooled their two boys, Kevin and Alex, from elementary through high school.

Upon graduation, both boys received four-year, full tuition scholarships from their first choice university. This enables Lee to pursue her dream job - helping parents homeschool their children through high school.

On The HomeScholar website, you will find great products for creating homeschool transcripts and comprehensive records to help you amaze and impress colleges.

Find out why Andrew Pudewa, Founder of the Institute for Excellence in Writing says, "Lee Binz knows how to navigate this often confusing and frustrating labyrinth better than anyone."

You can find Lee online at:

HomeHighSchoolHelp.com

If this book has been helpful, could you please take a minute to write us a quick review on Amazon?

Thank you!

Testimonials

I Recommend Her Highly

"If I could go back to the very, very beginning, and say to my wife, 'Sweetheart, I know this woman who will help you – let's just get her services and do this the easy way.' Lee is just one of the most encouraging and common sense, down to earth, but careful people in this whole business. I recommend her highly."

~ Andrew Pudewa, Director of the Institute for Excellence in Writing (IEW)

Easier and Less Stressful

"Thank you for all your help this year. My oldest child is a senior this year, about to graduate. We have always homeschooled him, along with our other children, but when he got ready to enter high school, it was a leap of faith whether to do it or not. I wasn't sure I could do it, and I was terrified he would never get into college. Although there are many homeschoolers in my area, most of the homeschoolers that I know either have kids that are younger than mine, or have decided against sending their children to college in the traditional way. Although we knew that our son was thinking about college, he was unsure of what he wanted to do.

Finally this past summer, the Lord spoke to his heart and my son started to make plans for attending college, except that we had no idea where to even start. We hadn't visited schools or even looked at them, we didn't have transcripts or course descriptions and no knowledge of how to apply for colleges, write college essays or apply for scholarships. In fact,

I was even behind on some of my grading because I had had a baby and had a toddler at home. All his high school papers were in piles in several different boxes with grades here and there. I felt completely overwhelmed and had no one to even ask for help. I had a couple of books that helped a little but I still had so many questions.

I had received your e-mails, and following you on Facebook but last fall I was finally able to attend one of your webinars. After the webinar I purchased the Comprehensive Record Solution and became a Gold Care Club member. Although I never taken advantage of your service on the phone or through e-mails, I did go through many of your materials. Although it took me months to get it all done, I did finally complete all of his transcripts, course descriptions, reading lists, activities, cover letters, etc. My son applied to four colleges, and was accepted to all and offered academic scholarships (not total scholarships, but every little bit helps!)

While he hasn't made a final decision, he has options, and that is in part because of your help. I was able to show in great detail all he had accomplished in an organized, easy to read and understand way. Thank you for all that you offer to homeschoolers, but especially to parents like me, that had no clue where to even begin. Although it was a tremendous amount of work, having all your wonderful help made it so much easier and less stressful. I thank the Lord that He led me to your site and all your outstanding knowledge. I recommend you to everyone that I speak to about this whole process and even listed your site as one of my favorite homeschooling helps at a recent support group meeting. Thank you for all that you have done."

~ Ms. Tiena

For more information about my **Total Transcript Solution** and **Comprehensive Record Solution**, go to:

www.TotalTranscriptSolution.com and www.ComprehensiveRecordSolution.com

Also From The HomeScholar...

- The HomeScholar Guide to College Admission and Scholarships: Homeschool Secrets to Getting Ready, Getting In and Getting Paid (Book and Kindle Book)
- Setting the Records Straight—How to Craft Homeschool Transcripts and Course Descriptions for College Admission and Scholarships (Book and Kindle Book)
- TechnoLogic: How to Set Logical Technology Boundaries and Stop the Zombie Apocalypse
- Finding the Faith to Homeschool High School
- The Easy Truth About Homeschool Transcripts (Kindle Book)
- Parent Training A la Carte (Online Training)

- Total Transcript Solution (Online Training, Tools and Templates)
- Comprehensive Record Solution (Online Training, Tools and Templates)
- Gold Care Club (Comprehensive Online Support and Training)
- Silver Training Club (Online Training)

The HomeScholar Coffee Break Books Released or Coming Soon on Kindle and Paperback:

- Delight Directed Learning: Guiding Your Homeschooler Toward Passionate Learning
- Creating Transcripts for Your Unique Child: Help Your Homeschool Graduate Stand Out from the Crowd
- Beyond Academics: Preparation for College and for Life
- Planning High School Courses: Charting the Course Toward High School Graduation
- Graduate Your Homeschooler in Style: Make Your Homeschool Graduation Memorable
- Keys to High School Success: Get Your Homeschool High School Started Right!

- Getting the Most Out of Your Homeschool This Summer: Learning just for the Fun of it!
- Finding a College: A Homeschooler's Guide to Finding a Perfect Fit
- College Scholarships for High School Credit: Learn and Earn With This Two-for-One Strategy!
- College Admission Policies Demystified: Understanding Homeschool Requirements for Getting In
- A Higher Calling: Homeschooling High School for Harried Husbands (by Matt Binz, Mr. HomeScholar)
- Gifted Education Strategies for Every Child: Homeschool Secrets for Success
- College Application Essays: A Primer for Parents
- Creating Homeschool Balance: Find Harmony Between Type A and Type Zzz...
- Homeschooling the Holidays: Sanity Saving Strategies and Gift Giving Ideas
- Your Goals this Year: A Year by Year Guide to Homeschooling High School
- Making the Grades: A Grouch-Free Guide to Homeschool Grading
- High School Testing: Knowledge That Saves Money

- Getting the BIG Scholarships: Learn Expert Secrets for Winning College Cash!
- Easy English for Simple Homeschooling: How to Teach, Assess and Document High School English
- Scheduling—The Secret to Homeschool Sanity: Plan You Way Back to Mental Health
- Junior Year is the Key to High School Success: How to Unlock the Gate to Graduation and Beyond
- Upper Echelon Education: How to Gain Admission to Elite Universities
- How to Homeschool College: Save Time, Reduce Stress and Eliminate Debt
- Homeschool Curriculum That's Effective and Fun: Avoid the Crummy Curriculum Hall of Shame!
- Comprehensive Homeschool Records: Put Your Best Foot Forward to Win College Admission and Scholarships
- Options After High School: Steps to Success for College or Career
- How to Homeschool 9th and 10th Grade: Simple Steps for Starting Strong!

- Senior Year Step-by-Step: Simple Instructions for Busy Homeschool Parents
- How to Homeschool Independently: Do-it-Yourself Secrets to Rekindle the Love of Learning
- High School Math The Easy Way: Simple Strategies for Homeschool Parents in Over Their Heads
- Homeschooling Middle School with Powerful Purpose: How to Successfully Navigate 6th through 8th Grade
- Simple Science for Homeschooling High School: Because Teaching Science isn't Rocket Science!

Would you like to be notified when we offer the next *Coffee Break Books* for FREE during our Kindle promotion days? If so, leave your name and email below and we will send you a reminder.

HomeHighSchoolHelp.com/ freekindlebook

Visit my Amazon Author Page!

amazon.com/author/leebinz

Made in the USA
Columbia, SC
24 January 2022